THE TRAIN OF STATES

Peter Sís

GREENWILLOW BOOKS
An Imprint of HarperCollinsPublishers

Library of Congress Cataloging-in-Publication Data

Sís, Peter.

The train of states / by Peter Sís.

  p. cm.

"Greenwillow Books."

Summary: Gives information about each state, including capital,
motto, state tree, state bird, source of name, and date of statehood.

ISBN 0-06-057838-6 (trade). ISBN 0-06-057839-4 (lib. bdg.)

1. U.S. states—Miscellanea—Juvenile literature. 2. United
States—Miscellanea—Juvenile literature. [1. U.S. states—
Miscellanea. 2. United States—Miscellanea.] I. Title.

E180.S58 2004 973'.02—dc22 2003056826

10 9 8 7 6 5 4 3 2 1

First Edition

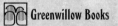

Greenwillow Books

*To twenty-two years in the United States
and twenty years with Greenwillow Books*

The Train of States is a personal journey that combines my love for my adopted country with my admiration for antique circus wagons. There are hundreds of facts, symbols, moments from history, tidbits, and details presented on these pages—many of them open to interpretation; several of them the topic of ongoing debate. I hope my book will lead you on your own journeys of discovery.

Very special thanks to Martha Mihalick and Anne Dunn, fact-checkers extraordinaire, and to Virginia Bartow of the Humanities and Social Sciences Library, The New York Public Library, for their relentless investigation of the materials presented in this book.

—PETER SÍS

"LIBERTY AND INDEPENDENCE"

PEACH BLOSSOM

AMERICAN HOLLY

SWEET GOLDENROD

LADYBUG

WEAKFISH

TIGER SWALLOWTAIL

BLUE HEN CHICKEN

FIRST STATE

DATE OF STATEHOOD

Named for Baron de la Warr, English governor of Virginia

Dover

American holly

peach blossom

blue hen chicken

In 1880, the first beauty contest in the U.S. was held in Rehoboth Beach. Thomas Edison was one of the three judges.

BENJAMIN FRANKLIN

HEMLOCK

HERSHEY'S KISS

RUFFED GROUSE

TRILOBITE

MOUNTAIN LAUREL

KEYSTONE STATE

GREAT DANE

BROOK TROUT

BETSY ROSS

MARIAN ANDERSON

FIRST LIBRARY

JAMES BUCHANAN

"VIRTUE, LIBERTY, AND INDEPENDENCE"

2. PENNSYLVANIA December 12, 1787

Named for Adm. Sir William Penn and the Latin *silva*, meaning "woodland"

 Harrisburg

 hemlock

When legislators made the Great Dane the state dog in 1965, they voted with yips, growls, and barks.

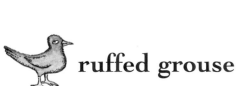 mountain laurel

ruffed grouse

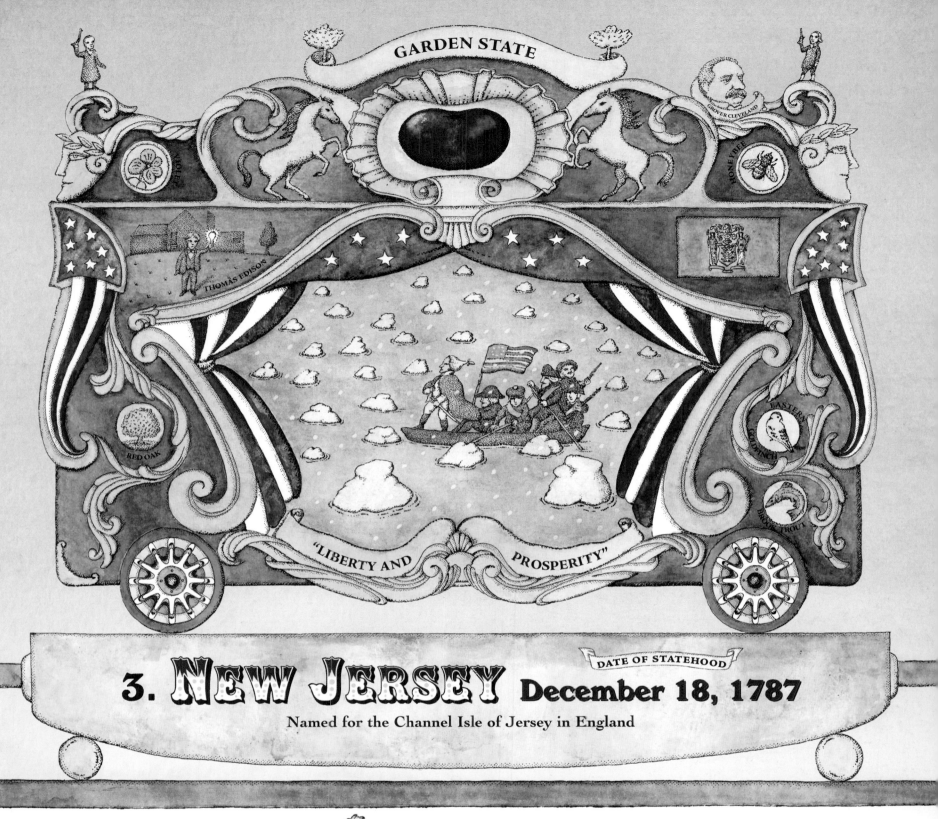

GARDEN STATE

GROVER CLEVELAND

THOMAS EDISON

"LIBERTY AND PROSPERITY"

DATE OF STATEHOOD

3. NEW JERSEY December 18, 1787

Named for the Channel Isle of Jersey in England

 Trenton

 red oak

 violet

 eastern goldfinch

The "Bone Wars"—a bitter feud between paleontologists—began in New Jersey ten years after the first nearly complete dinosaur skeleton was found there in 1858.

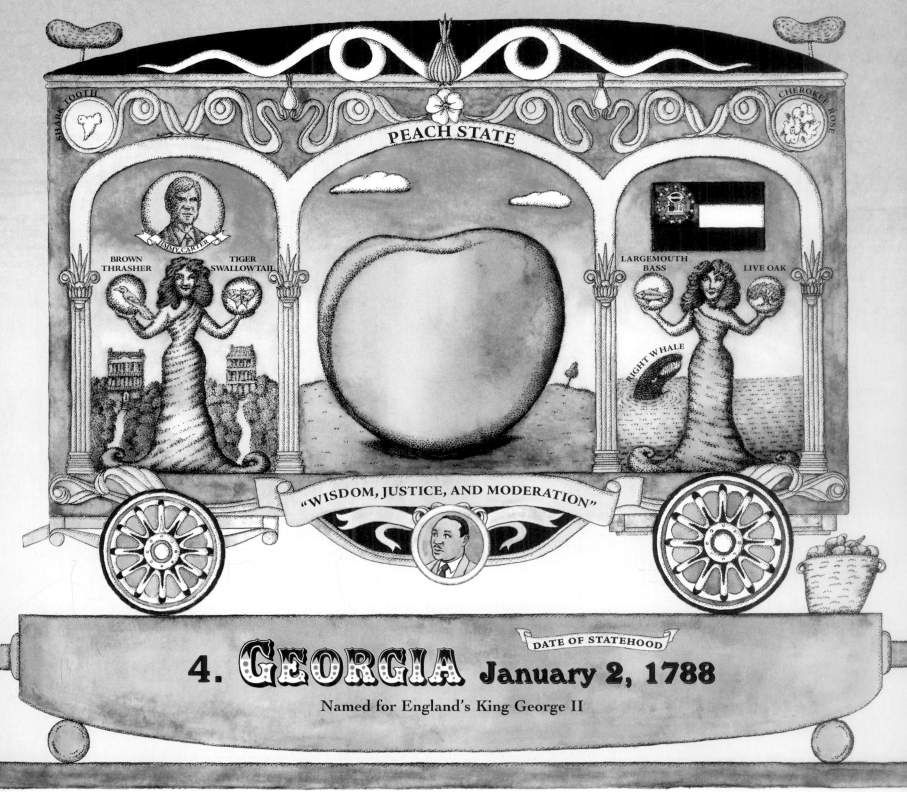

PEACH STATE

SHARK TOOTH

CHEROKEE ROSE

JIMMY CARTER

BROWN THRASHER

TIGER SWALLOWTAIL

LARGEMOUTH BASS

LIVE OAK

RIGHT WHALE

"WISDOM, JUSTICE, AND MODERATION"

DATE OF STATEHOOD

4. GEORGIA January 2, 1788

Named for England's King George II

 Atlanta

Cherokee rose

live oak

brown thrasher

Civil rights activist and Atlanta native Martin Luther King, Jr., was born Michael Luther King; he was renamed when he was six.

CONSTITUTION STATE

AMERICAN ROBIN

MOUNTAIN LAUREL

YANKEE DOODLE

P. T. BARNUM

WHITE OAK

OYSTERS

GEORGE W. BUSH

"HE WHO TRANSPLANTED STILL SUSTAINS"

DATE OF STATEHOOD

5. CONNECTICUT January 9, 1788

Named for the Mohegan Indian *quinnehtukqut*, meaning "beside the long tidal river."

 Hartford

 white oak

 mountain laurel

American robin

The first hamburger was served in 1895 at Louie's Lunch in New Haven.

MASSASOIT
TURKEY
BLACK-CAPPED CHICKADEE

BAY STATE

PHILLIS WHEATLEY
LOUISA MAY ALCOTT

JOHN ADAMS
JOHN QUINCY ADAMS
JOHN F. KENNEDY
GEORGE H. W. BUSH

PAUL REVERE

AMERICAN ELM
MAYFLOWER
NEPTUNE SHELL
NORTHERN RIGHT-WHALE
LADYBUG
ALEXANDER GRAHAM BELL
CAPE COD
COD

BOSTON TERRIER
MORGAN HORSE

"BY THE SWORD WE SEEK PEACE,
BUT PEACE ONLY UNDER LIBERTY"

DATE OF STATEHOOD

6. MASSACHUSETTS February 6, 1788

Named for the Algonquian Indian word meaning "at the big hill"

 Boston

 American elm

 mayflower

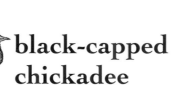 black-capped chickadee

In 1891, James Naismith invented the game of basketball in Springfield. The first game was played with a soccer ball and peach baskets hung ten feet in the air.

FIRST REFRIGERATOR

BALTIMORE CHECKERSPOT

HARRIET TUBMAN

KING WILLIAM'S SCHOOL

STRIPED BASS

WHITE OAK

DIAMONDBACK TERRAPIN

BLACK-EYED SUSAN

BALTIMORE ORIOLE

OLD LINE STATE

CALICO CAT

CHESAPEAKE BAY RETRIEVER

"MANLY DEEDS, WOMANLY WORDS"

DATE OF STATEHOOD

7. MARYLAND April 28, 1788

Named for Henrietta Maria, queen to England's Charles I

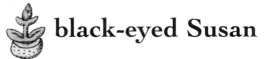 Annapolis

white oak

black-eyed Susan

Baltimore oriole

Francis Scott Key wrote "The Star-Spangled Banner" from a British ship in the Baltimore harbor in 1814.

PALMETTO STATE

ANDREW JACKSON

BLUE GRANITE

PEACH

EASTERN TIGER SWALLOWTAIL

YELLOW JESSAMINE

SPOTTED SALAMANDER

CAROLINA WREN

BOYKIN SPANIEL

"PREPARED IN MIND AND RESOURCES"
"WHILE I BREATHE, I HOPE"

DATE OF STATEHOOD

8. SOUTH CAROLINA May 23, 1788

Named for England's King Charles I

 Columbia

palmetto

 yellow jessamine

 Carolina wren

South Carolina is considered to have some of the most pristine nesting areas for loggerhead sea turtles, a threatened species.

GRANITE STATE

"LIVE FREE OR DIE"

9. **NEW HAMPSHIRE**

DATE OF STATEHOOD
June 21, 1788

Named for Hampshire County, England

 Concord

 white birch

 purple lilac

 purple finch

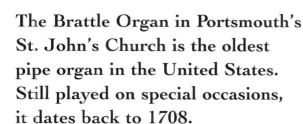 The Brattle Organ in Portsmouth's St. John's Church is the oldest pipe organ in the United States. Still played on special occasions, it dates back to 1708.

GEORGE WASHINGTON · THOMAS JEFFERSON · JAMES MADISON · JAMES MONROE · WILLIAM HENRY HARRISON · JOHN TYLER · ZACHARY TAYLOR · WOODROW WILSON

CARDINAL

BROOK TROUT

"THUS ALWAYS TO TYRANTS"

MOUNT VERNON

MONTICELLO

TIGER SWALLOWTAIL

DOGWOOD

POCAHONTAS

OLD DOMINION STATE

DATE OF STATEHOOD

10. VIRGINIA June 25, 1788

Named for England's Queen Elizabeth I, the Virgin Queen

 Richmond

 dogwood

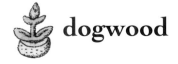 dogwood

 cardinal

Both the Revolutionary War and the Civil War ended in Virginia, the first in Yorktown in 1781 and the second at Appomattox Court House in 1865.

EMPIRE STATE

ROSE BROOK TROUT PRETZEL

BLUEBIRD SUGAR MAPLE

FRANKLIN D. ROOSEVELT

THEODORE ROOSEVELT

SUSAN B. ANTHONY

MARTIN VAN BUREN

MILLARD FILLMORE

"EVER UPWARD"

SOJOURNER TRUTH

ELEANOR ROOSEVELT

11. NEW YORK July 26, 1788

DATE OF STATEHOOD

Named for England's Duke of York

 Albany

 rose

sugar maple

bluebird

Chittenango, birthplace of *The Wizard of Oz* author L. Frank Baum, has a yellow brick road and an annual Munchkin parade.

ANDREW JOHNSON

JAMES POLK

GREAT SMOKY MOUNTAINS

BLUEBERRY   CARDINAL   DOGWOOD   CHANNEL BASS   PINE   PLOTT HOUND

TAR HEEL STATE

FIRST GOLD NUGGET

EASTERN BOX TURTLE

"TO BE RATHER THAN TO SEEM"

12. NORTH CAROLINA

DATE OF STATEHOOD

November 21, 1789

Named for England's King Charles I

 Raleigh

 dogwood

pine

 cardinal

The Roanoke Island colony vanished between 1587, when leader John White went back to England for supplies, and 1590, when he returned. The only clue was the word "Croatoan" carved into a tree.

RED MAPLE

GREENING APPLE

RHODE ISLAND RED

VIOLET

STRIPED BASS

OCEAN STATE

OLDEST SCHOOLHOUSE

OLDEST CAROUSEL

FIRST CIRCUS

"HOPE"

DATE OF STATEHOOD

13. RHODE ISLAND May 29, 1790

Named for the Greek island of Rhodes

 Providence

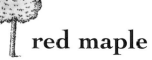 red maple

The Flying Horse Carousel in Watch Hill is the oldest carousel in the U.S. in continuous operation.

 violet

 Rhode Island red

CHESTER ARTHUR

CALVIN COOLIDGE

"FREEDOM AND UNITY"

WALLEYE PIKE

BROOK TROUT

HERMIT THRUSH

HONEYBEE

MONARCH

SUGAR MAPLE

RED CLOVER

NORTHERN LEOPARD FROG

MAPLE SYRUP

MORGAN HORSE

GREEN MOUNTAIN STATE

DATE OF STATEHOOD

14. **VERMONT** March 4, 1791

Named for the French words *vert mont*, meaning "green mountain"

 Montpelier

 sugar maple

 red clover

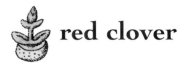 hermit thrush

 Vermont's was the first state constitution to outlaw slavery—in 1777.

BLUEGRASS MUSIC

ABRAHAM LINCOLN

BLUEGRASS STATE

CARDINAL

KENTUCKY BASS

VICEROY

MAMMOTH CAVE

BEAGLE

GRAY SQUIRREL

GOLDENROD

TULIP TREE

"UNITED WE STAND, DIVIDED WE FALL"

15. **KENTUCKY** June 1, 1792

DATE OF STATEHOOD

Named for the Iroquois Indian word meaning "land of tomorrow"

 Frankfort

 tulip tree

 goldenrod

 cardinal

More than six billion dollars' worth of gold is held in the underground vaults of Fort Knox. This is the largest amount of gold stored anywhere in the world.

VOLUNTEER STATE

MOCKINGBIRD

ZEBRA SWALLOWTAIL

ELVIS PRESLEY

FIRST U.S. GUIDE DOG

CHANNEL CATFISH

LARGEMOUTH BASS

BOX TURTLE

LIGHTNING BUG

TULIP TREE

IRIS

RACCOON

AGRICULTURE AND COMMERCE

DATE OF STATEHOOD

16. TENNESSEE June 1, 1796

Named for *Tanasi,* an important Cherokee Indian village

  Nashville

 tulip tree

iris

 mockingbird

 Morris Frank from Nashville was the first American to use a guide dog for the blind. His dog, Buddy, was a female German shepherd he brought home from a guide dog school in Switzerland.

17. **OHIO** March 1, 1803

DATE OF STATEHOOD

Named for the Iroquois Indian word *oheo*, meaning "great river"

 Columbus

buckeye

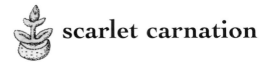 scarlet carnation

cardinal

In 1879, Cleveland became the first city in the U.S. to have electric street lamps.

PELICAN STATE

BALD CYPRESS · CATAHOULA LEOPARD DOG · MAGNOLIA · IRIS · BLACK BEAR · ACCORDION

NEW ORLEANS

BROWN PELICAN

ALLIGATOR

"UNION, JUSTICE, AND CONFIDENCE"

DATE OF STATEHOOD

18. LOUISIANA April 30, 1812

Named for King Louis XIV of France

 Baton Rouge

bald cypress

magnolia

brown pelican

The town of Jean Lafitte is named after the legendary buccaneer and veteran of the Battle of New Orleans and War of 1812.

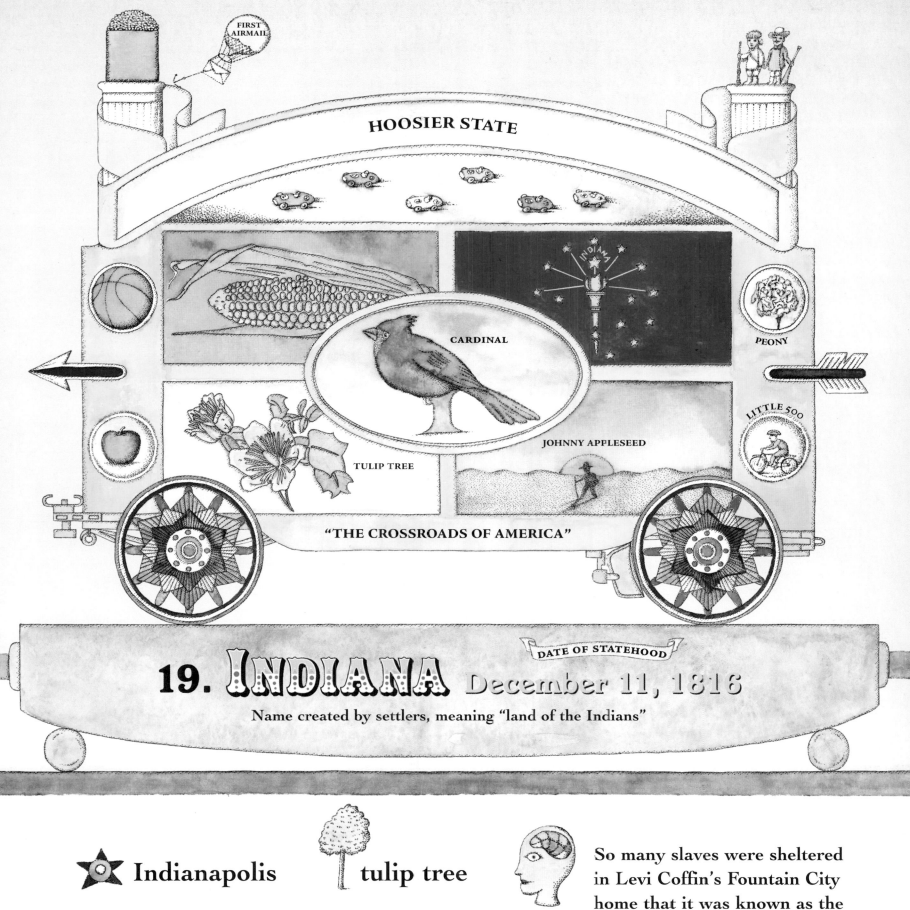

FIRST AIRMAIL

HOOSIER STATE

CARDINAL

PEONY

TULIP TREE

JOHNNY APPLESEED

LITTLE 500

"THE CROSSROADS OF AMERICA"

DATE OF STATEHOOD

19. INDIANA December 11, 1816

Name created by settlers, meaning "land of the Indians"

Indianapolis

tulip tree

peony

cardinal

So many slaves were sheltered in Levi Coffin's Fountain City home that it was known as the "Grand Central Station" of the Underground Railroad.

PUSHMATAHA

HONEYBEE

SPICEBUSH SWALLOWTAIL

MAGNOLIA STATE

MAGNOLIA

THE BLUES

MOCKINGBIRD

WOOD DUCK

LARGEMOUTH BASS

"BY VALOR AND ARMS"

DATE OF STATEHOOD

20. MISSISSIPPI December 10, 1817

Named for the Chippewa Indian words *mici zibi*, meaning "great river"

 Jackson

magnolia

 magnolia

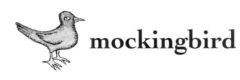 mockingbird

On May 11, 1887, a 6 x 8 inch gopher turtle completely encased in ice fell from the sky during a severe hailstorm near Bovina.

PRAIRIE STATE

RONALD REAGAN

ILLINOIS

MONARCH

WHITE OAK

BLUEGILL

"STATE SOVEREIGNTY NATIONAL UNION"

CHICAGO

CARDINAL

WHITE-TAILED DEER

VIOLET

ABRAHAM LINCOLN

21. ILLINOIS December 3, 1818

DATE OF STATEHOOD

Named for a French corruption of the Algonquian Indian word meaning "superior men"

 Springfield

 white oak

 violet

 cardinal

The Home Insurance Building in Chicago was the world's first modern skyscraper. It was 138 feet high.

HELEN KELLER

ROSA PARKS

HEART OF DIXIE

CAMELLIA

LARGEMOUTH BASS

FIGHTING TARPON

RED-BELLIED TURTLE

SOUTHERN LONGLEAF PINE

RACKING HORSE

MONARCH

YELLOWHAMMER

WILD TURKEY

"WE DARE DEFEND OUR RIGHTS"

DATE OF STATEHOOD

22. ALABAMA December 14, 1819

Name may be from the Alibamu Indians, members of the Creek Confederacy.
Possibly from the Choctaw language, *alba ayamule*, meaning "I clear the thicket."

Montgomery

southern longleaf pine

Rosa Parks refused to give up her seat on a city bus in 1955, which began the Montgomery bus boycott.

camellia

yellowhammer

PINE TREE STATE

HONEYBEE

CHICKADEE

WINTERGREEN

MAINE COON CAT

WHITE PINE CONE & TASSEL

WILD BLUEBERRY

LANDLOCKED SALMON

"I LEAD"

DATE OF STATEHOOD

23. MAINE March 15, 1820

Name may have originated from explorers referring to the "mainland," from a province in northwestern France, or from a town on the coast of England

 Augusta

 white pine

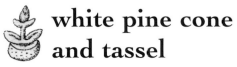 white pine cone and tassel

 chickadee

Margaret Chase Smith of Skowhegan became the first woman to serve in both houses of Congress when she was elected to the Senate in 1948.

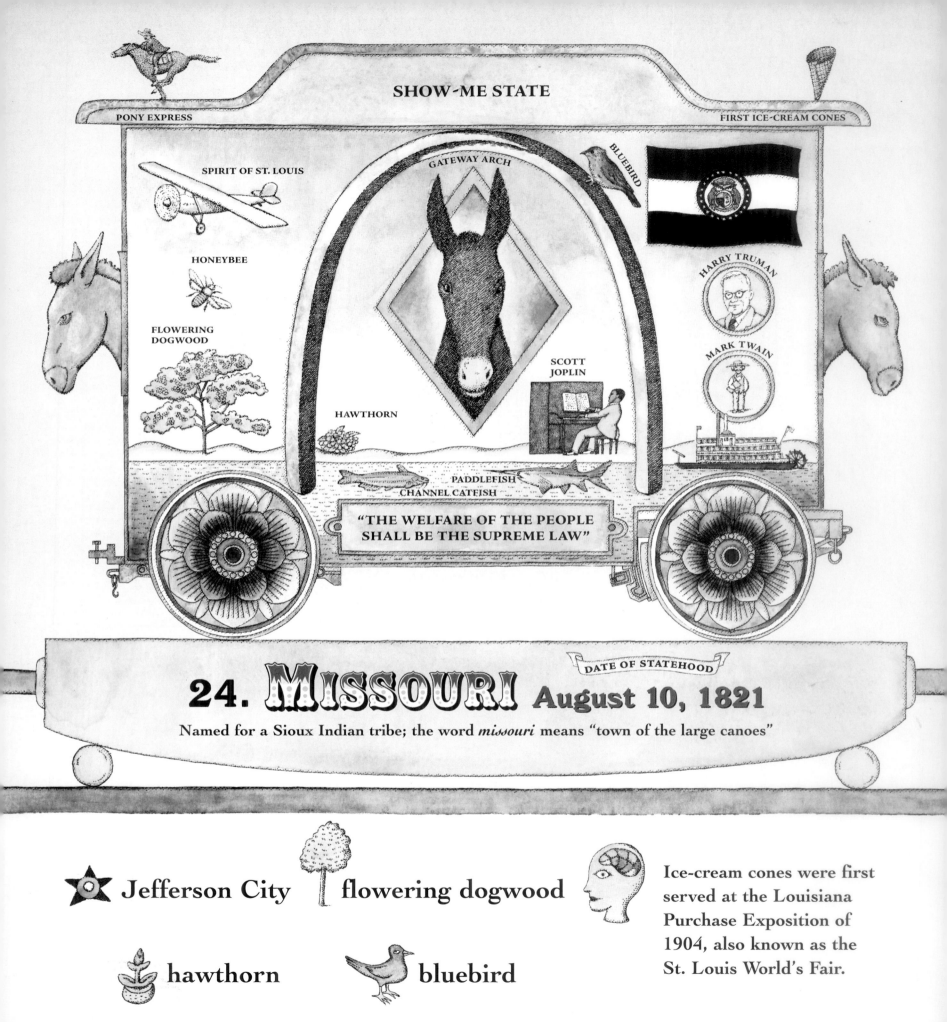

PONY EXPRESS

SHOW-ME STATE

FIRST ICE-CREAM CONES

SPIRIT OF ST. LOUIS

GATEWAY ARCH

BLUEBIRD

HONEYBEE

FLOWERING DOGWOOD

HARRY TRUMAN

SCOTT JOPLIN

MARK TWAIN

HAWTHORN

PADDLEFISH

CHANNEL CATFISH

"THE WELFARE OF THE PEOPLE SHALL BE THE SUPREME LAW"

DATE OF STATEHOOD

24. MISSOURI August 10, 1821

Named for a Sioux Indian tribe; the word *missouri* means "town of the large canoes"

Jefferson City

flowering dogwood

hawthorn

bluebird

Ice-cream cones were first served at the Louisiana Purchase Exposition of 1904, also known as the St. Louis World's Fair.

NATURAL STATE

MOCKINGBIRD

WILLIAM J. CLINTON

SOUTH ARKANSAS VINE

RIPE PINK TOMATO

HONEYBEE

PINE

APPLE BLOSSOM

WHITE-TAILED DEER

"THE PEOPLE RULE"

DATE OF STATEHOOD

25. ARKANSAS June 15, 1836

Named for the Quapaw Indians, who were called Akansea, meaning "south wind," by other tribes

Little Rock

pine

apple blossom

mockingbird

The World's Championship Duck Calling Contest is held annually in Stuttgart.

GREAT LAKE STATE

ANTOINE DE LA MOTHE CADILLAC

"IF YOU SEEK A PLEASANT PENINSULA, LOOK ABOUT YOU"

APPLE BLOSSOM

WHITE PINE

ROBIN

BROOK TROUT

DWARF LAKE IRIS

WHITE-TAILED DEER

PAINTED TURTLE

DATE OF STATEHOOD

26. MICHIGAN January 26, 1837

Named for the Algonquian Indian word *michigama*, meaning "great lake"

 Lansing

white pine

 apple blossom

 robin

 In 1866 James Vernor of Detroit created his recipe for ginger ale, the first soft drink made in the U.S.

ORANGE BLOSSOM

MOCKINGBIRD

SUNSHINE STATE

KENNEDY SPACE CENTER

SABAL PALM

PONCE DE LEON'S EXPEDITION

LARGEMOUTH BASS

SAILFISH

HORSE CONCH

"IN GOD WE TRUST"

PANTHER

ALLIGATOR

DATE OF STATEHOOD

27. FLORIDA March 3, 1845

Named for Pascua Florida, the Spanish Eastertime "Feast of Flowers," by the explorer Ponce de Leon

⭐ Tallahassee

🌳 sabal palm

About one million alligators live in the state of Florida.

🌱 orange blossom

🐦 mockingbird

LONE STAR STATE

ARMADILLO

HORNED LIZARD

DWIGHT D. EISENHOWER

LYNDON B. JOHNSON

"FRIENDSHIP"

DATE OF STATEHOOD

28. TEXAS December 29, 1845

Named for the Caddo Indian word *tejas*, meaning "friends" or "allies"

 Austin

 pecan

 bluebonnet

 mockingbird

In 1856, Jefferson Davis had camels imported to transport military provisions across west Texas. The Camel Corps had mixed success and ended in 1861.

"OUR LIBERTIES WE PRIZE, AND OUR RIGHTS WE WILL MAINTAIN"

HERBERT HOOVER

GEODE

EASTERN GOLDFINCH

WILD ROSE

HAWKEYE STATE

OAK

ANTONÍN DVOŘÁK

DATE OF STATEHOOD

29. IOWA December 28, 1846

Named for the Iowa Indians

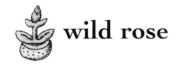 Des Moines

 oak

 wild rose

 eastern goldfinch

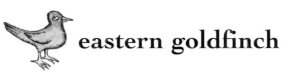 Every year since 1960, the Iowa State Fair has featured a 600-pound butter sculpture of a dairy cow.

BADGER STATE

WISCONSIN
1848

HARRY HOUDINI

FRANK LLOYD WRIGHT

AMERICAN WATER SPANIEL

GENERAL MACARTHUR

TRILOBITE

GREEN BAY PACKERS

DAIRY COW

ROBIN

HONEYBEE

SUGAR MAPLE

WOOD VIOLET

MUSKELLUNGE

"FORWARD"

30. WISCONSIN May 29, 1848

DATE OF STATEHOOD

Named for the French version of a Chippewa Indian term meaning "grassy place"

⭐ Madison

🌳 sugar maple

🌱 wood violet

🐦 robin

Every year the Great Circus Parade—a re-creation of the old-time street parades of wagons, animals, and performers—rolls through downtown Milwaukee.

GOLDEN STATE

"EUREKA"

31. CALIFORNIA September 9, 1850

DATE OF STATEHOOD

Named for an island paradise in a popular Spanish novel from around 1510

 Sacramento

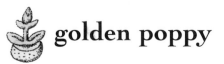 golden poppy

California redwood

California quail

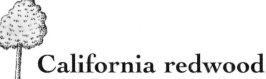 The first blue jeans were created in 1853 by Levi Strauss and became the uniform for gold prospectors.

PINK AND WHITE LADY'S SLIPPER

RED PINE

NORTH STAR

STATE

MOREL

MONARCH

WALLEYE

TWIN CITIES

COMMON LOON

"THE STAR OF THE NORTH"

DATE OF STATEHOOD

32. MINNESOTA May 11, 1858

Named for the Dakota Indian word meaning "sky-tinted water"

 St. Paul

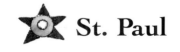 red pine

 pink and white lady's slipper

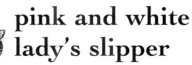 common loon

 The 130-feet-tall ice palace constructed for the 1888 St. Paul Winter Carnival was by far the city's tallest building at the time.

BEAVER STATE

"SHE FLIES WITH HER OWN WINGS"

WESTERN MEADOWLARK

OREGON GRAPE

DOUGLAS FIR

OREGON SWALLOWTAIL

HAZELNUT

CHINOOK SALMON

CHIEF JOSEPH

PACIFIC GOLDEN CHANTERELLE

STATE OF OREGON
1855

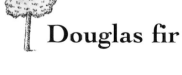

33. OREGON February 14, 1859

DATE OF STATEHOOD

The origins of "Oregon" are uncertain, but it was likely derived from an Indian word.

 Salem

Douglas fir

 Oregon grape

western meadowlark

Formed more than 7,000 years ago, Crater Lake is the deepest lake in the U.S., with an average depth of 1,500 feet and a maximum depth of 1,949 feet.

"TO THE STARS THROUGH DIFFICULTIES"

WESTERN MEADOWLARK

ORNATE BOX TURTLE

COTTONWOOD

NATIVE SUNFLOWER

BARRED TIGER SALAMANDER

CHANNEL CATFISH

HONEYBEE

KANSAS

SUNFLOWER STATE

DATE OF STATEHOOD

34. KANSAS January 29, 1861

Named for the Kansa Indians; *kansa* means "people of the south wind"

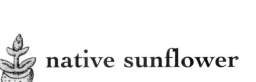 Topeka

cottonwood

 native sunflower

western meadowlark

The geographic center of the continental 48 United States is located in Smith County, near Lebanon, in north-central Kansas.

GOLDEN DELICIOUS APPLE

MOUNTAIN STATE

THOMAS "STONEWALL" JACKSON

BROOK TROUT

CARDINAL

MONARCH

SUGAR MAPLE

HONEYBEE

RHODODENDRON

ORGAN CAVE

"MOUNTAINEERS ARE ALWAYS FREE"

DATE OF STATEHOOD

35. WEST VIRGINIA — June 20, 1863

Named for England's Queen Elizabeth I, the Virgin Queen

 Charleston

sugar maple

 rhododendron

 cardinal

The continent's largest conical burial mound is in Moundsville. It is 69 feet high and 295 feet in diameter.

SILVER STATE

MOUNTAIN BLUEBIRD

DESERT TORTOISE

TURQUOISE

SINGLE-LEAF PIÑON

LAHONTAN CUTTHROAT TROUT

DESERT BIGHORN SHEEP

SAGEBRUSH

BRISTLECONE PINE

"ALL FOR OUR COUNTRY"

DATE OF STATEHOOD

36. NEVADA October 31, 1864

Named for the Spanish word *nevada*, meaning "snow-capped"

 Carson City

 single-leaf piñon and bristlecone pine

 sagebrush

 mountain bluebird

 Hard hats were first invented in 1933 specifically for workers on the Hoover Dam, the largest single public works project of its day.

CORNHUSKER STATE

COTTONWOOD

WESTERN MEADOWLARK

WHITE-TAILED DEER

CHANNEL CATFISH

HONEYBEE

GERALD FORD

MAMMOTH

GOLDENROD

BLUE CHALCEDONY

"EQUALITY BEFORE THE LAW"

DATE OF STATEHOOD

37. NEBRASKA March 1, 1867

Named for the Oto Indian word *nebrathka*, meaning "flat water"

 Lincoln

cottonwood

 goldenrod

western meadowlark

The longest porch swing in the world is in Hebron. It can seat eighteen adults or twenty-four children.

CENTENNIAL STATE

"NOTHING WITHOUT THE DEITY"

BLUE GRAMA GRASS

BLUE SPRUCE

WHITE AND LAVENDER COLUMBINE

HAIRSTREAK

GREENBACK CUTTHROAT TROUT

LARK BUNTING

38. COLORADO August 1, 1876

DATE OF STATEHOOD

Named for the Spanish word *colorado*, meaning "red" or "ruddy"

 Denver

blue spruce

 white and lavender columbine

lark bunting

After gold was discovered near Pikes Peak in 1858, the slogan "Pikes Peak or Bust" began appearing painted on prairie schooners (the covered wagons used by pioneers).

PEACE GARDEN STATE

NORTHERN PIKE

AMERICAN ELM

NOKOTA

WESTERN MEADOWLARK

INTERNATIONAL PEACE GARDEN

SACAGAWEA

WILD PRAIRIE ROSE

THEODORE ROOSEVELT

"LIBERTY AND UNION, NOW AND FOREVER, ONE AND INSEPARABLE"

39. NORTH DAKOTA
November 2, 1889

DATE OF STATEHOOD

Named for the Sioux Indian word *dakota*, meaning "friend"

Bismarck

American elm

wild prairie rose

western meadowlark

North Dakota has 63 National Wildlife Refuges, more than any other state.

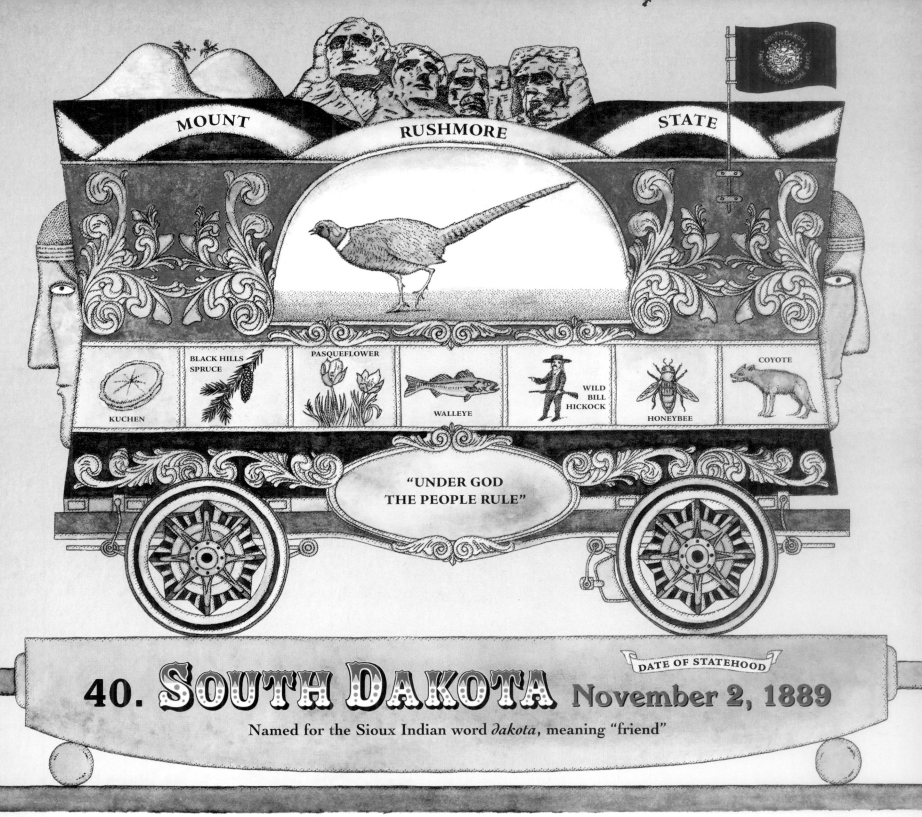

MOUNT RUSHMORE STATE

KUCHEN

BLACK HILLS SPRUCE

PASQUEFLOWER

WALLEYE

WILD BILL HICKOCK

HONEYBEE

COYOTE

"UNDER GOD
THE PEOPLE RULE"

40. SOUTH DAKOTA November 2, 1889

DATE OF STATEHOOD

Named for the Sioux Indian word *dakota*, meaning "friend"

 Pierre

 pasqueflower

Black Hills spruce

ring-necked pheasant

 Sue, the largest and most intact *T. rex* fossil, was discovered by Sue Hendrickson in 1990 near the town of Faith.

BIG SKY COUNTRY

WESTERN MEADOWLARK

MOURNING CLOAK

TREASURE STATE

PONDEROSA PINE

MONTANA

BITTERROOT

"GOLD AND SILVER"

BLACKSPOTTED CUTTHROAT TROUT

DATE OF STATEHOOD

41. MONTANA November 8, 1889

Named for the Latin *montaanus*, meaning "mountainous"

Helena

Ponderosa pine

In Montana elk, deer, and antelope outnumber humans.

bitterroot

western meadowlark

STEELHEAD TROUT

EVERGREEN STATE

AMERICAN GOLDFINCH

APPLE

GREEN DARNER DRAGONFLY

PETRIFIED WOOD

"BY AND BY"

COAST RHODODENDRON

THE SEAL OF THE STATE OF WASHINGTON 1889

WESTERN HEMLOCK

42. WASHINGTON November 11, 1889

DATE OF STATEHOOD

Named for George Washington, the first U.S. president

 Olympia

western hemlock

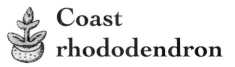 Coast rhododendron

 American goldfinch

 In 1980, Mount St. Helens, a volcano in the Cascade Range that had been dormant since 1857, erupted in one of the biggest volcanic disturbances in U.S. history.

GEM STATE

MONARCH

IDAHO STAR GARNET

MOUNTAIN BLUEBIRD

SYRINGA

WESTERN WHITE PINE

HUCKLEBERRY

CUTTHROAT TROUT

"LET IT BE PERPETUAL"

DATE OF STATEHOOD

43. IDAHO July 3, 1890

Name was coined or invented, and was originally used for a Columbia River steamship

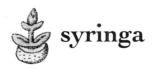 Boise

western white pine

 syringa

 mountain bluebird

The state capitol building in Boise is heated by underground hot springs.

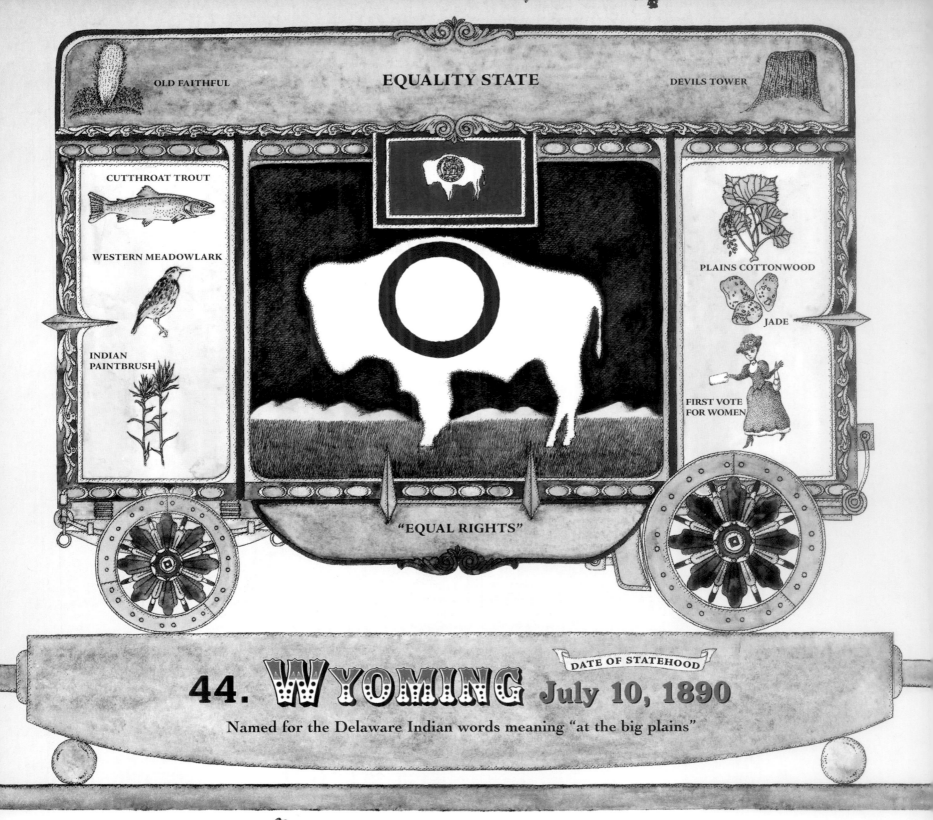

EQUALITY STATE

OLD FAITHFUL

DEVILS TOWER

CUTTHROAT TROUT

WESTERN MEADOWLARK

INDIAN PAINTBRUSH

PLAINS COTTONWOOD

JADE

FIRST VOTE FOR WOMEN

"EQUAL RIGHTS"

DATE OF STATEHOOD

44. WYOMING July 10, 1890

Named for the Delaware Indian words meaning "at the big plains"

 Cheyenne plains cottonwood

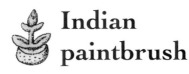 Indian paintbrush  western meadowlark

Thousands of people traveling west on the Oregon Trail scratched their names on the surface of Independence Rock, which sits fifty miles southwest of Casper.

INDIAN RICE GRASS

BEEHIVE STATE

SEGO LILY

CALIFORNIA GULL

BLUE SPRUCE

BONNEVILLE

CUTTHROAT TROUT

DUBHE

TOPAZ

CHERRY

ROCKY MOUNTAIN ELK

"INDUSTRY"

DATE OF STATEHOOD

45. UTAH January 4, 1896

Named for the Ute Indians (people of the mountains)

Salt Lake City

blue spruce

sego lily

California gull

Great Salt Lake is the fourth largest terminal (no outlet) lake in the world, three to five times saltier than the ocean, and free of fish (the largest marine creatures are brine shrimp).

SOONER STATE

BULL FROG

COLLARED LIZARD

BLACK SWALLOWTAIL

MISTLETOE

INDIAN BLANKET

FIDDLE

WHITE BASS

REDBUD

OKLAHOMA

"LABOR CONQUERS ALL THINGS"

SCISSOR-TAILED FLYCATCHER

DATE OF STATEHOOD

46. OKLAHOMA November 16, 1907

Named for the Choctaw Indian words meaning "red people"

Oklahoma City

redbud

mistletoe

scissor-tailed flycatcher

Oklahoma has the only state capitol building in the world with an oil well drilled beneath it.

LAND OF ENCHANTMENT

GEORGIA O'KEEFFE

TARANTULA HAWK WASP

BLACK BEAR

PIÑON

"IT GROWS AS IT GOES"

CUTTHROAT TROUT

YUCCA

47. NEW MEXICO January 6, 1912

DATE OF STATEHOOD

Named by Spanish explorers, for Mexico

Santa Fe

piñon

yucca

roadrunner

The city of Santa Fe was settled in 1607, making it the oldest state capital city in the country.

GRAND CANYON STATE

CACTUS WREN

APACHE TROUT

SAGUARO CACTUS BLOSSOM

GRAND CANYON

PALO VERDE

ARIZONA TREE FROG

TWO-TAILED SWALLOWTAIL

ARIZONA RIDGENOSE RATTLESNAKE

GERONIMO

"GOD ENRICHES"

48. ARIZONA February 14, 1912

DATE OF STATEHOOD

Named for the Papago Indian word *arizonac*, meaning "place of the small spring"

 Phoenix

palo verde

 blossom of the saguaro cactus

cactus wren

In 1930, Clyde Tombaugh at Lowell Observatory in Flagstaff discovered the planet Pluto.

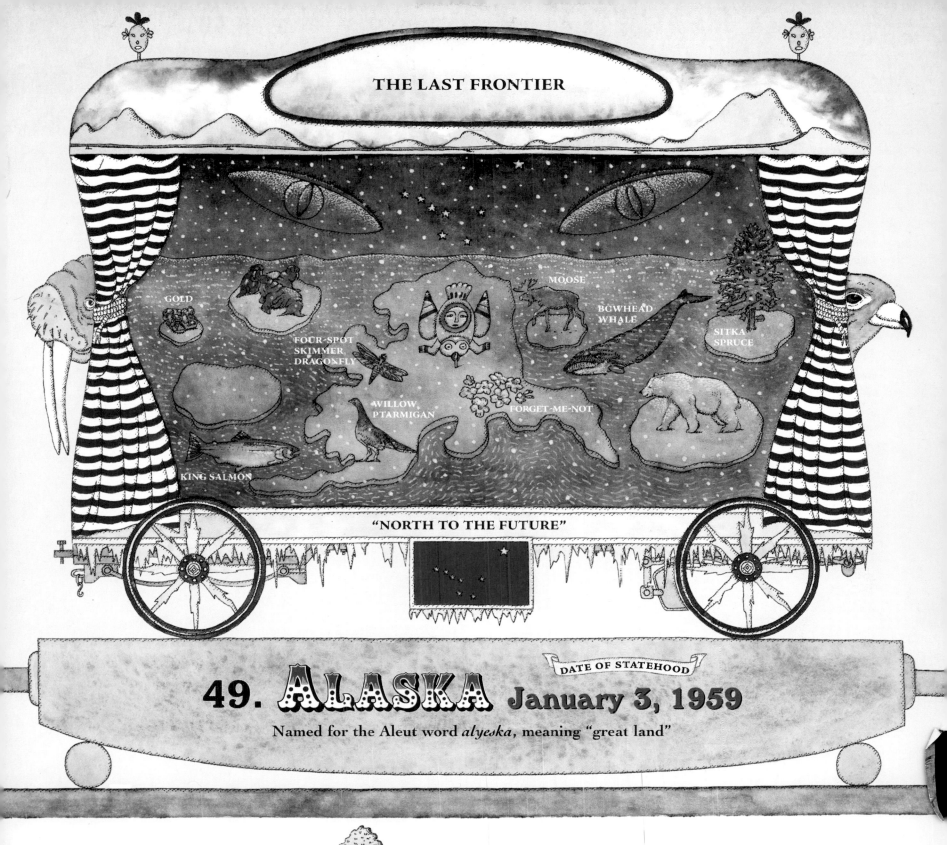

THE LAST FRONTIER

GOLD

FOUR-SPOT
SKIMMER
DRAGONFLY

MOOSE

BOWHEAD
WHALE

SITKA
SPRUCE

WILLOW
PTARMIGAN

FORGET-ME-NOT

KING SALMON

"NORTH TO THE FUTURE"

DATE OF STATEHOOD

49. ALASKA January 3, 1959

Named for the Aleut word *alyeska*, meaning "great land"

 Juneau

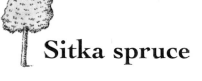 Sitka spruce

 forget-me-not

 willow ptarmigan

In Barrow, Alaska's northernmost point, the sun doesn't set for 84 days during the summer months.

NENE

KILAUEA

HALEAKALA

BLACK CORAL

QUEEN LILIUOKALANI

HUMPBACK WHALE

HAWAIIAN TRIGGERFISH

ALOHA STATE

YELLOW HIBISCUS

CANDLENUT

"THE LIFE OF THE LAND IS PERPETUATED IN RIGHTEOUSNESS"

DATE OF STATEHOOD

50. HAWAII August 21, 1959

Named for the Polynesian word *hawaiki*, meaning "homeland"

Honolulu

candlenut

yellow hibiscus

nene

Honolulu's Iolani Palace is the only royal residence in the U.S.

"JUSTICE FOR ALL"

SCARLET OAK

WHITE HOUSE

WASHINGTON MONUMENT

WOOD THRUSH

CAPITOL

AMERICAN BEAUTY ROSE

LINCOLN MEMORIAL

WASHINGTON, D.C. July 16, 1790

Named in honor of George Washington and Christopher Columbus (District of Columbia)

The capital of the U.S.

American Beauty rose

scarlet oak

wood thrush

The Supreme Court has its own independent police force, which is responsible for a one-block area.

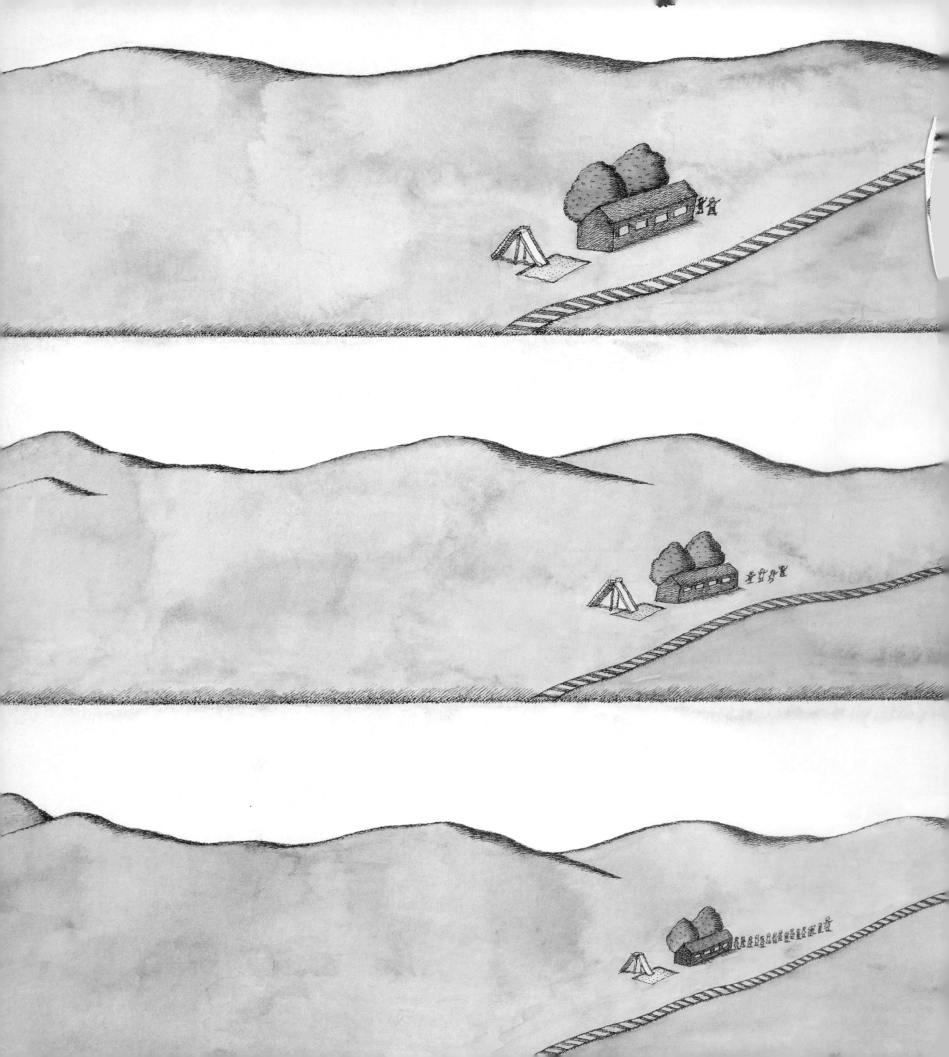

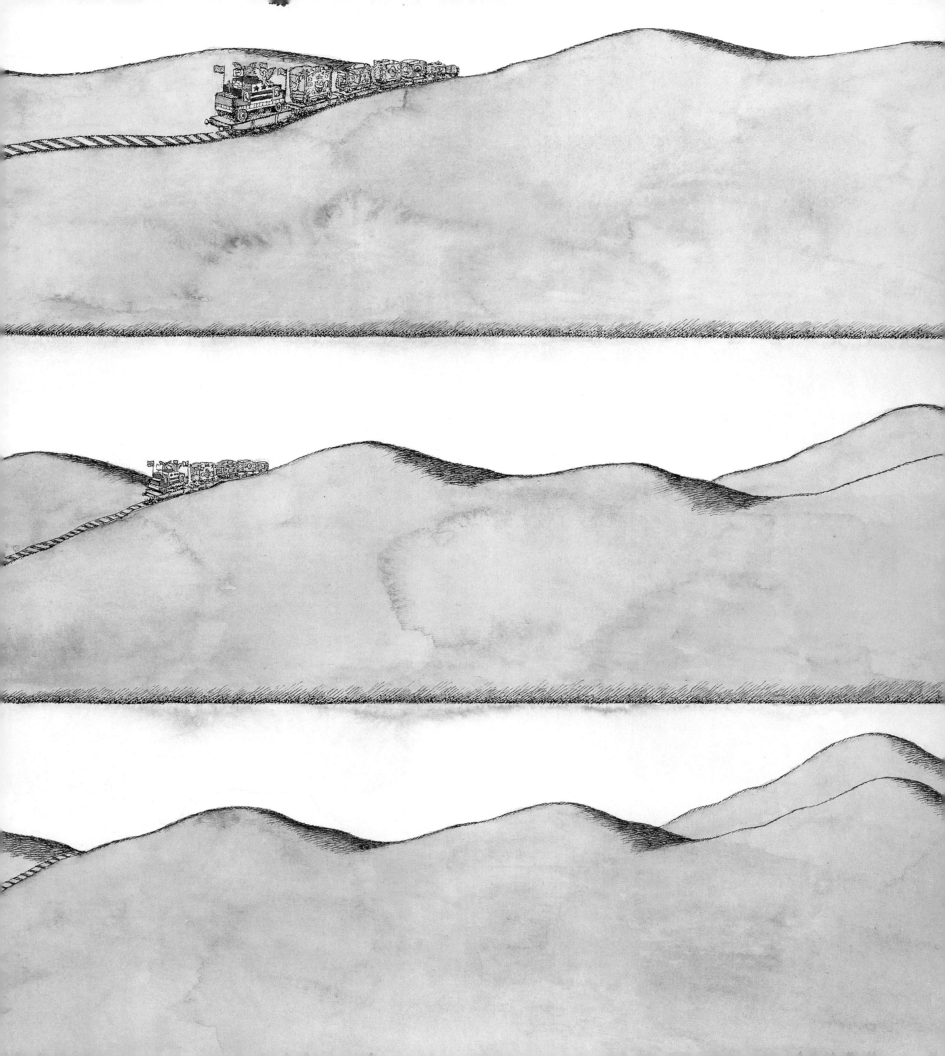

A note about the illustrations in this book

KEY:

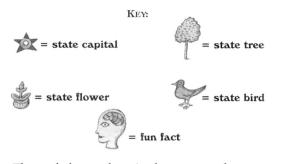

★ = state capital

= state tree

= state flower

= state bird

= fun fact

The symbols, people, animals, scenes, and designs on each wagon are pictured for a reason. Look for the story behind each picture. Visit your library and the Internet and talk to your parents, relatives, teachers, and friends to learn more about the states. If you created your own train of states, what would you draw on each wagon? Here are some leads to get you started:

1. **DELAWARE:** Can you find a diamond on this wagon? Thomas Jefferson nicknamed Delaware "The Diamond State" in tribute to its small size but great strategic value.

2. **PENNSYLVANIA:** Binney & Smith invented Crayola Crayons in Easton in 1903. • Why is Benjamin Franklin pictured with a kite and key? • Did you know that Benjamin Franklin established the first library in the colonies?

3. **NEW JERSEY:** Can you spot George Washington? • Why are Aaron Burr and Alexander Hamilton dueling?

4. **GEORGIA:** The official state vegetable of Georgia is the sweet Vidalia onion. Can you find it here? • Georgia is the top producer of peanuts and peaches in the U.S.

5. **CONNECTICUT:** The Naval Submarine Base New London was the Navy's first submarine base.

6. **MASSACHUSETTS:** Can you spot Plymouth Rock? • The Boston Tea Party took place on December 16, 1773. • Who is standing to the left of the striped flag?

7. **MARYLAND:** King William's School opened in 1696. • The wild horses of Assateague Island are the size of ponies.

8. **SOUTH CAROLINA:** The "Best Friend of Charleston" (1830) was the first steam locomotive in the U.S. to offer a scheduled service for passengers.

9. **NEW HAMPSHIRE:** No two Concord Coaches were ever the same. Custom-painted and famous for comfort, these stagecoaches were built by the Abbot, Downing Company in Concord. Can you spot one here?

10. **VIRGINIA:** The Chesapeake Bay Bridge-Tunnel is 18 miles long and is the longest bridge-tunnel complex in the world. • The Virginia House of Delegate's Mace symbolizes the importance of government. Can you find it?

11. **NEW YORK:** Can you spot Niagara Falls? • Peter Sís, the author of this book, lives near Sunnyside, Washington Irving's home. Can you find two of Irving's creations here? • Fact or fiction: Peter Minuit bought Manhattan in 1626. • The last rivet on the Statue of Liberty was put into place in 1886.

12. **NORTH CAROLINA:** First flight! On December 17, 1903, the Wright brothers, Orville (right) and Wilbur, made three short flights at Kill Devil Hills, near Kitty Hawk. • Did you know that the first gold nugget in the U.S. was found in 1799 in Cabarrus County?

13. **RHODE ISLAND:** Newport was the site of the first circus in the U.S., in 1774. • Newport was founded in 1639 and was one of the busiest ports in the colonies.

14. **VERMONT:** Elisha Graves Otis, inventor of the elevator brake, was born near Halifax. Look for his name the next time you ride an elevator!

15. **KENTUCKY:** Abraham Lincoln and Jefferson Davis, key leaders of the Union and Confederacy, were born within nine months of each another and less than one hundred miles apart. Can you spot them here?

16. **TENNESSEE:** The Grand Ole Opry has been broadcasting live on the radio since 1925. Can you spot the musicians here? • Tennessee has more than 3,800 caves. • Davy Crockett was born August 17, 1786. His rifle was named "Old Betsy." • The state commercial fish is the channel catfish; the state game fish is the largemouth bass. What is the difference?

17. **OHIO:** Neil Armstrong was born August 5, 1930; John Glenn was born July 18, 1921. • The flying pigs on top of steamboat smokestacks guarding the entrance to Cincinnati's Bicentennial Commons recall a time when the city was nicknamed Porkopolis, a reference to the meat packing industry.

18. **LOUISIANA:** The St. Louis Cathedral was built in 1718. Can you find it? • The first Mardi Gras parade took place in New Orleans in 1857. • The Mississippi River reaches the Gulf of Mexico just south of New Orleans.

19. **INDIANA:** How long is the Indianapolis 500? • Indiana is one of the top five popcorn-producing states in the U.S. • On October 26, 1803, Meriwether Lewis and William Clark and the first members of the Corps of Discovery began their journey of exploration from the Falls of the Ohio, near Clarksville.

20. **MISSISSIPPI:** When President Theodore Roosevelt refused to shoot a bear cub near Onward, Morris Michtom stuffed a toy bear and called it "Teddy's Bear." • The slouch hat, originally a civilian hat, became part of the official uniform of the Confederate army during the Civil War.

21. **ILLINOIS:** Can you spot Ida B. Wells and Jane Addams? • The Sears Tower in Chicago was the tallest building in the world from 1973 to 1996.

22. **ALABAMA:** Why is cotton pictured here?

23. **MAINE:** August is Maine Lobster Month. • There are more than sixty lighthouses along Maine's coast.

24. **MISSOURI:** The Missouri River—"Big Muddy"—flows 2,315 miles before joining the Mississippi just north of St. Louis.

25. **ARKANSAS:** What is an Arkansan? • The nation's only active diamond mine is located near Murfreesboro.

26. **MICHIGAN:** Henry Ford and his son Edsel were both born in Michigan. • Pictured here is a 1916 Ford Model T.

27. **FLORIDA:** Florida has coastline on both the Atlantic Ocean and the Gulf of Mexico.

28. **TEXAS:** The battle of the Alamo took place in San Antonio, then called Bejar, in 1836. • The Lady Bird Johnson Wildflower Center is in Austin.

29. **IOWA:** The Red Delicious apple, originally grown near Peru by James (Jesse) Hiatt in the late 1800s, is one of the world's most popular varieties.

30. **WISCONSIN:** Magician Harry Houdini called Appleton his hometown, but he was really born in Budapest, Hungary.

31. **CALIFORNIA:** Gold was discovered at Sutter's Mill on January 24, 1848, and the California Gold Rush began.

32. **MINNESOTA:** Did you know that there are actually more than 15,000 lakes in the "Land of 10,000 Lakes?" • Sod houses, or "soddies," such as the one pictured here were made of layers of turf bricks. Could that be Laura Ingalls Wilder in the doorway?

33. **OREGON:** Mount Hood, a volcano in the Cascade Range, last erupted in 1805, just before the arrival of Lewis and Clark on October 18.

34. **KANSAS:** Amelia Earhart was born on July 24, 1897, in Atchison.

35. **WEST VIRGINIA:** Spruce Knob in the Appalachian Mountains is the highest point in the state. How high is it?

36. **NEVADA:** Camels were imported to Nevada in the 1850s and used as pack animals.

37. **NEBRASKA:** Nebraska is also called "The Tree Planter's State." • The state tree is the cottonwood; cottonwood trees were often landmarks for the pioneers.

38. **COLORADO:** The Great Sand Dunes National Monument & Preserve has dunes over 750 feet high.

39. **NORTH DAKOTA:** Black-tailed prairie dogs usually live in enormous "towns" covering one hundred or more acres.

40. **SOUTH DAKOTA:** Can you spot Sitting Bull and Crazy Horse? • Can you find Presidents Washington, Jefferson, Roosevelt, and Lincoln?

41. **MONTANA:** The Battle of the Little Bighorn (also known as Custer's Last Stand) was fought on June 25, 1876.

42. **WASHINGTON:** Can you spot Chief Seattle?

43. **IDAHO:** The russet Burbank (a potato introduced by Luther Burbank in 1872) is Idaho's most famous potato.

44. **WYOMING:** Wyoming is called the Equality State because it was the first state to give women the right to vote. Laramie's Louisa "Grandma" Swain cast the first ballot in 1870. • Is a bison the same thing as a buffalo?

45. **UTAH:** On May 10, 1869, lines constructed by the Central Pacific and Union Pacific Railroads were joined in Promontory by the Golden Spike, forming the first transcontinental railroad in the U.S.

46. **OKLAHOMA:** The Five Civilized Tribes were the Cherokee, Chickasaw, Choctaw, Creek, and Seminole.

47. **NEW MEXICO:** The Pueblo of Acoma is also known as Sky City because it's atop a 357-foot-tall mesa. • An international balloon festival takes place in Albuquerque every autumn.

48. **ARIZONA:** What do Gila monsters eat? • More than four million people visit the Grand Canyon National Park each year.

49. **ALASKA:** The Alaskan pipeline is 800 miles long. • How big is Alaska?

50. **HAWAII:** The Hawaiian Triggerfish is also called the humuhumunukunukuapua`a.

THE CABOOSE: WASHINGTON, D.C.: You can register to vote when you turn 18.